A Day in the Life of a
CHAMELEON
A 4D BOOK

by Lisa J. Amstutz

Consultant: Robert T. Mason
Professor of Integrative Biology
J.C. Braly Curator of Vertebrates
Oregon State University

PEBBLE
a capstone imprint

Download the Capstone 4D app!

- Ask an adult to download the Capstone 4D app.

- Scan the cover and stars inside the book for additional content.

When you scan a spread, you'll find
fun extra stuff to go with this book!
You can also find these things
on the web at www.capstone4D.com
using the password: chameleon.31756

A+ Books are published by Pebble
1710 Roe Crest Drive, North Mankato, Minnesota 56003
www.mycapstone.com

Library of Congress Cataloging-in-Publication Data
Names: Amstutz, Lisa J., author.
Title: A day in the life of a chameleon : a 4D book / by Lisa J. Amstutz.
Description: North Mankato, Minnesota : an imprint of Pebble, [2019] |
   Series: A+ books. A day in the life | Audience: Age 4–8.
Identifiers: LCCN 2018006118 (print) | LCCN 2018009145 (ebook) |
   ISBN 9781543531770 (eBook PDF) | ISBN 9781543531756 (library binding) |
   ISBN 9781543531763 (paperback)
Subjects: LCSH: Chameleons—Life cycles—Juvenile literature.
Classification: LCC QL666.L23 (ebook) | LCC QL666.L23 A47 2019 (print) |
   DDC 597.95/6156—dc23
LC record available at https://lccn.loc.gov/2018006118

Editorial Credits
Gina Kammer, editor; Jennifer Bergstrom, designer;
Morgan Walters, media researcher; Laura Manthe, production specialist

Photo Credits
Alamy: FLPA, 22; Getty Images: Wolfgang Kaehler, 21; iStockphoto: Alan_Lagadu, 7; Newscom:
Vincent Grafhorst/ Minden Pictures, 20; Shutterstock: Ava Peattie, 23, Cathy Keifer, 15, 29, Eileen
Kumpf, 10, Hugh Lansdown, 4, Jan Bures, Cover, 11, 16, 27, Jason Mintzer, 9, 18, 19, KonKoratio, 17,
Maris Pukitis, 25, Peter Krejzl, 1, Petr Kovalenkov, 26, Pierre-Yves Babelon, 5, Robert Fowler, 8, 30,
SaveJungle, Cover, design element througout, Vaclav Sebek, 12, 13, Vladislav T. Jirousek, 24, Zaruba
Ondrej, 14

Note to Parents, Teachers, and Librarians

This book uses full color photographs and a nonfiction format to introduce the concept of a
chameleon's day. *A Day in the Life of a Chameleon* is designed to be read aloud to a pre-reader or to
be read independently by an early reader. Photographs help listeners and early readers understand
the text and concepts discussed. The book encourages further learning by including the following
sections: Table of Contents, Glossary, Read More, Internet Sites, Critical Thinking Questions, and
Index. Early readers may need assistance using these features.

Printed in the United States of America.
PA017

TABLE OF CONTENTS

A Chameleon's Day 4

Life Cycle of a
Panther Chameleon 30

Glossary 31

Read More 31

Internet Sites 31

Critical Thinking
Questions 32

Index 32

A Chameleon's Day

At the end of a branch, a panther chameleon sleeps. He looks safe and snug. But danger hides in the night. Rats, snakes, and other predators are on the hunt. If the chameleon feels the branch move, he will drop to safety.

Sun rays stretch across the sky. They warm the chameleon. He is cold-blooded. He needs heat from the sun to warm up. The chameleon lives in Madagascar, a country in Africa. He spends most of his life in trees and bushes.

The chameleon is hungry. He looks for food. His scaly eyes are shaped like cones. He looks through a small hole at the end. The chameleon can look two different ways at once. He can even see behind him!

LOOK!

Look! A cricket is sitting under a leaf. The chameleon slowly moves closer.

The lizard's five toes clamp onto the
branch. They grab it like a hand.

The chameleon is near his prey.
He stops and wraps his tail around
the branch. It helps him hold on.
The chameleon must take good care
of his tail. Unlike other lizards, he
cannot lose and regrow it.

SHLIP!

SHLIP! The chameleon's long, sticky tongue shoots out. It is as long as his body! He stores it at the back of his throat.

The end of the chameleon's tongue hits his prey and sticks. *ZAP!* He pulls the bug back into his mouth.

ZAP!

CRUNCH! The chameleon's strong jaws crush
the cricket. Insects are his favorite food.

As the chameleon rests, he looks around.
Uh-oh! He spots another male nearby.
He puffs out his throat and his body.
His skin begins to change color. A bright
pattern appears. It tells the other male
to stay out of the chameleon's territory.
The other male moves on.

UH-OH!

The chameleon changes colors
when he is scared or mad. Light
and heat can make him change
colors too.

The chameleon has four layers of skin. Cells in the second and third layer contain pigments. These color cells can shrink or grow. The changes in size make different colors show.

19

The chameleon spots a flash of color
overhead. What's that? It's a female!
At 10 inches (25 centimeters) long,
she is about half his size. Her colors
are not as bright as his. But they're
still beautiful. She uses her colors to
talk to him.

COLORS!

The chameleons mate. Two to three weeks later, the female will climb down the tree. She will dig a hole and lay eggs. She will cover them with leaves and dirt to hide them.

The young will hatch out in a few months. Young chameleons look like tiny adults. They are the size of a dime. They start hunting right away. Their parents do not feed them.

As the young grow, they shed their skin.
It comes off in patches. They keep growing
all of their lives.

Watch out! A predator is near. It is a hungry bird. The chameleon sits very still. He blends in with the leaves on the tree. The bird does not see him. It flies on. That was close!

The chameleon crawls to a new branch. He will look for insects here. He licks drops of rain from a branch.

As night falls, the forest grows quiet. The chameleon creeps to the end of his branch and hugs it. He closes his eyes to sleep.

Good night, chameleon!

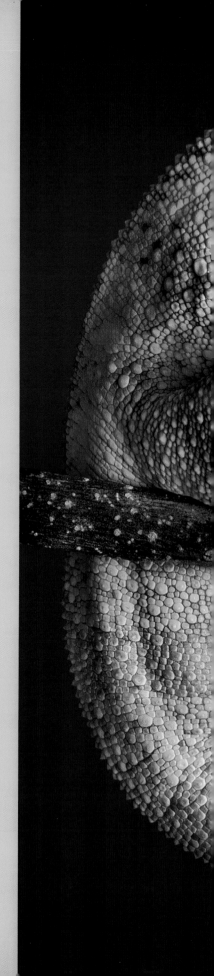

LIFE CYCLE OF A
PANTHER
CHAMELEON

1

Female panther chameleons lay eggs in the ground. In **6** to **12 MONTHS,** her young hatch out.

2

The **YOUNG CHAMELEONS** start hunting right away. Their parents do not feed them.

3

The **YOUNG LIZARDS** grow fast. They shed their skin as they grow.

4

At **FIVE MONTHS OLD,** the young lizards find mates of their own.

Glossary

cell—a basic part of an animal or plant that is so small you can't see it without a microscope

cold-blooded—having a body temperature that changes with the surroundings

mate—to join together to produce young; a mate is also the male or female partner of a pair of animals

pattern—a repeated design of colors

pigment—a substance that gives something a particular color when it is present in it or is added to it

predator—an animal that hunts other animals for food

prey—an animal hunted by another animal for food

territory—an area of land that an animal claims as its own to live in

Read More

Bodden, Valerie. *Chameleons.* Amazing Animals. Mankato, Minn.: Creative Education/ Creative Paperbacks, 2016.

Marsico, Katie. *Chameleons Change Color.* Ann Arbor, Mich.: Cherry Lake Publishing, 2016.

Statts, Leo. *Chameleons.* Zoom in on Desert Animals. Minneapolis: Abdo Zoom, 2017.

Internet Sites

Use FactHound to find Internet sites related to this book.

Visit *www.facthound.com*

Just type in 9781543531756 and go.

Check out projects, games and lots more at
www.capstonekids.com

Critical Thinking Questions

1. How do chameleons hunt?

2. What makes chameleons change colors?

3. Where do chameleons sleep, and why?

4. How might having eyes that can look in different directions help chameleons?

Index

Africa, 6

birds, 24

colors, 16, 18, 19, 20

crickets, 10, 15

eggs, 21

eyes, 8, 28

food, 8, 15

growing, 23

hunting, 4, 14, 22

jaws, 15

Madagascar, 6

predators, 4, 24

prey, 12, 14

rats, 4

shedding, 23

skin, 16, 19, 23

sleeping, 4, 28

snakes, 4

tails, 12

toes, 11

tongues, 13, 14